PROFESSIONAL ENGLISH II

MS M SARANYA & MRS M LINJU

Contents

Preface

In today's globalized world, proficiency in English is no longer optional—it is essential for professional growth, effective communication, and cross-cultural collaboration. This textbook is designed to equip learners with the tools they need to navigate the demands of professional environments with confidence and fluency.

This book adopts a practical approach to learning professional English, emphasizing real-world applications and interactive exercises. Whether you are preparing resumes, writing formal emails, participating in meetings, or negotiating in a multicultural workplace, the lessons within are structured to enhance both your language skills and cultural awareness.

This textbook is intended for professionals, students, and anyone seeking to refine their English proficiency in business and professional contexts. It is suitable for learners at intermediate to advanced levels, with clear explanations and activities that challenge users to apply what they learn.

The content of this book remains relevant, engaging, and aligned with the evolving demands of the professional world. Hope the learning and teaching community will get some benefits out of this book in enhancing the employability quotient. At the same time, we fondly expect to have your constructive criticism to improve this piece of work.

Prologue

In today's interconnected world, mastering English is more than just a valuable skill—it is a necessity. Whether you are negotiating deals, delivering presentations, writing reports, or participating in global discussions, the ability to communicate clearly and confidently in English can open doors to opportunities that transcend borders.

Throughout this journey, you will discover techniques to improve your business writing, strategies to enhance your verbal communication, and insights into the cultural nuances that influence professional interactions. From mastering email etiquette to handling challenging conversations, this book offers practical guidance that is immediately applicable.

The purpose of this book is not just to teach English but to empower you with the tools to make a lasting impression in professional settings. With each chapter, you will build confidence, precision, and adaptability, equipping you to navigate complex scenarios and leave a positive impact.

As you embark on this journey, remember that professional English is not just about language; it's about connection, clarity, and influence. Let this book be your guide to unlocking your full potential in the world of professional communication.

Contents

Authors

Ms. Saranya M
MA, (PhD)
Assistant Professor
Department of English
Nehru Arts and Science College, Thirumalayampalayam
Coimbatore, Tamil Nadu

Ms Saranya M serves as an Assistant Professor of English at Nehru Arts and Science College, Coimbatore. She holds a Master's degree in English and is currently pursuing her PhD at Bharathiar University. A dedicated researcher, she has published papers in esteemed national and international journals. Her areas of specialization include Indian Literature, War Literature, and Mythological Narratives. In addition to her academic qualifications, she has completed several online courses to further enhance her expertise. As an academician, she has undertaken various responsibilities, such as serving as the Fine Arts Club Coordinator and Placement Coordinator, as well as being an active member of the Exam Cell. She has also contributed to skill development by teaching courses on Public Speaking, Employability Skills, and Communication Skills.

Mrs. Linju M
MA, M Phil, (PhD)
Assistant Professor
Department of English
Nehru Arts and Science College, Thirumalayampalayam
Coimbatore, Tamil Nadu

Mrs. Linju M is currently working as an Assistant Professor at Nehru Arts and Science College, Thirumalayampalayam, Coimbatore. Her qualifications are MA, MPhil and PhD ongoing in Bharathiar University. She has published papers in international journals and national journals and presented papers in international conferences. Her areas of specialisation are Indian Literature, American Literature and Eco fiction. She has taught diverse subjects in literature for both undergraduate and post graduate levels. She has also taught Soft Skills, Personality Development and facilitated placement readiness classes, guiding students through resume building, communication skills, and industry-specific recruitment processes.

ONE

WOMEN NOT WEAKER SEX

· MAHATMA GANDHI

If I was born a woman, I would rise in rebellion against any pretension on the part of man that woman is born to be his plaything. I have mentally become a woman in order to steal into her heart. I could not steal into my wife's heart until I decided to treat her differently than I used to do, and so I restored to her all her today as simple as myself. You find no necklaces, no fineries, and the slaves of men. Refuse to decorate yourselves, and don't go in for scents and lavender waters. If you (women) want to give out the proper scent it must come out of your heart, and then you will captivate not man, but humanity. It is your birth-right. Man is born of woman; he is flesh of her flesh and bone of her bone. Come to your own and deliver your message again.

Woman must cease to consider herself the object of man's lust. The remedy is more in her hands than man's. She must refuse to adorn herself for men, including her husband, if she will be an equal partner with man. I cannot imagine Sita wasting even a single moment on pleasing Rama by physical charms.

Of all the evils for which man has made himself responsible, none is so degrading, so shocking or so brutal as his abuse of the better half of humanity. To me, the female sex, is not the weaker sex. It is the nobler of the two, for it is even today the embodiment of sacrifice, silent suffering, humility, faith and knowledge.

Woman, I hold, is the personification of self-sacrifice, but unfortunately today she does not realize what a tremendous advantage she has over man. As Tolstoy used to say, they are laboring under the hypnotic influence of man. If they would realize the strength of non-violence, they would not consent to be called the weaker sex.

To call woman the weaker sex is a libel; it is man's injustice to woman. If by strength is meant brute strength, then indeed, is woman less brute than man. If by strength is meant moral power, then woman is immeasurably man's superior. Has she not greater intuition, is she not greater courage? Without her man could not be. If non-violence is the law of our being. The future is with woman....... Who can make a more effective appeal to the heart than woman?

Had not man in his blind selfishness crushed woman's soul as he has done or had she not succumbed to 'the enjoyments' she would have given the world an exhibition of the infinite strength that is latent in her. The world shall see it in all its wonder and glory when woman has secured an equal opportunity for herself with man and fully developed her power of mutual aid and combination.

Women are special custodians of all that is pure and religious in life. Conservative by nature, if they are slow to shed superstitious habits, they are also slow to give up all that is pure and noble in life.

I am uncompromising in the matter of women's rights. In my opinion she should labour under no legal disability not suffered by man. I should treat daughters and sons on a footing of perfect equality.

I believe in the proper education of women. But I do believe that woman will not make her contribution to the world by mimicking or running a race with man. She can run the race, but she will not rise to the great heights she is capable of by mimicking man. She has to be the complement of man.

Glossary:

1. Pretension- An attempt to appear more important, knowledgeable, or sophisticated than one truly is.
2. Brute Strength- Raw, physical power or force.
3. **Patriarchy**- A social system where men hold primary power, dominating roles in political leadership, moral authority, and control of property.
4. Empowerment- The process of becoming stronger and more confident, especially in controlling one's life and claiming one's rights.

5. Endurance- The capacity to endure hardships or suffering with patience and perseverance.

Notes:

Mahatma Gandhi's essay "Women Are Not the Weaker Sex" challenges traditional societal norms that view women as inferior to men. It appears in his collection **The Mind of Mahatma Gandhi.** In this piece, Gandhi challenges the traditional notion that women are the weaker sex, arguing instead for their strength, resilience, and essential role in society. He argues for gender equality and highlights the immense strength, courage, and moral power of women, often overlooked in patriarchal societies. Below is a detailed summary and exploration of the key themes for a three-page understanding.

Summary of "Women Are Not the Weaker Sex"
Introduction

- **Challenging Stereotypes**: Gandhi begins by addressing the prevalent view that women are weaker than men, physically, emotionally, and intellectually. He asserts that this belief is baseless and a product of social conditioning rather than reality.
- **Inherent Strength**: Gandhi argues that women possess inner strength and resilience, often far superior to that of men. He cites examples from Indian mythology, culture, and history to show that women have always played vital roles in society but have been subjugated due to patriarchal structures.

Moral Strength of Women

- **Non-violence and Endurance**: According to Gandhi, women are naturally more inclined towards nonviolence (ahimsa) and possess the ability to endure suffering with greater calmness and strength than men. He connects this to the idea of satyagraha (nonviolent resistance), a principle central to his philosophy.
- **Motherhood and Sacrifice**: Gandhi highlights the role of women as mothers and caregivers, emphasizing their capacity for love, sacrifice, and nurturing. He argues that these qualities, far from making women weaker, reflect their immense inner power and moral strength.

Women in Indian Society

- **Historical Figures**: Gandhi draws on examples of women from India's history and culture, such as Sita, Draupadi, and Queen Ahilyabai, to demonstrate the leadership, courage, and resilience of women. These figures, Gandhi suggests, should serve as role models for modern women.
- **Social Inequality**: He criticizes the social structures that have confined women to limited roles, blaming both men and women for perpetuating these conditions. He calls for a radical change in societal attitudes toward gender.

Women in the Freedom Struggle

- **Role in the Independence Movement**: Gandhi highlights the significant contributions of women in India's freedom struggle. From participating in protests and boycotts to making personal sacrifices, women demonstrated courage and commitment to the cause of national liberation.
- **Empowerment Through Satyagraha**: Gandhi asserts that women were natural satyagrahis because of their capacity for self-control, patience, and nonviolence. He encourages them to embrace their strength and participate fully in the movement for freedom and equality.

Call for Gender Equality

- **Equal Rights**: Gandhi advocates for equal opportunities for women in all spheres of life, including education, employment, and politics. He argues that a society cannot progress if half of its population is denied the opportunity to reach its full potential.
- **Breaking the Chains of Patriarchy**: He calls on both men and women to challenge the traditional notions of gender roles. Men must stop treating women as inferiors, and women must realize their own power and worth.

Key Themes
Inner Strength vs. Physical Power

- Gandhi contrasts the notion of physical strength, typically associated with men, with the inner strength of women, which he views as far superior. He emphasizes that physical might is not the only measure of strength and that emotional resilience, moral courage, and the ability to endure suffering are forms of strength often possessed by women.
- This theme is significant as it redefines the concept of strength, moving away from brute force to qualities like patience, compassion, and perseverance.

Nonviolence and Women's Role in Satyagraha

- Gandhi aligns the principle of nonviolence (ahimsa) with women's natural disposition. He believes that women, through their patience, sacrifice, and nurturing spirit, are better suited for satyagraha than men. This theme highlights how Gandhi sees women as crucial to the success of his nonviolent resistance movement.
- He also suggests that women's ability to endure and forgive is an essential aspect of the moral struggle for justice.
-

Empowerment through Education and Participation

- A significant part of Gandhi's argument is that women must be empowered through education and active participation in societal and political life. He believes that only through education can women break free from the chains of ignorance and subjugation.
- Gandhi emphasizes that women have the capacity to contribute meaningfully to society and that their empowerment is essential for the nation's progress.

Gender Equality

- Gandhi's message is clear: women are equal to men in every aspect and must be given the same opportunities and rights. He opposes the traditional patriarchal notion that women should be confined to the home or relegated to secondary roles in society.
- This theme of gender equality is central to Gandhi's vision for a just and equitable society. He sees the liberation of women as essential to India's

overall progress and independence.

Role of Women in Nation Building

- Gandhi strongly believes that women have a crucial role to play in the nation's development. He argues that the participation of women in the independence movement is symbolic of their broader role in nation-building.
- This theme reflects Gandhi's forward-thinking approach to women's empowerment, advocating for their leadership in public and political life.

Conclusion

In "Women Are Not the Weaker Sex," Mahatma Gandhi presents a powerful argument for the strength and equality of women, urging society to abandon outdated gender stereotypes. He envisions a world where women and men work together as equals, contributing to the moral and social progress of the nation. Gandhi's message remains relevant today as the struggle for gender equality continues in many parts of the world.

The essay serves not only as a critique of patriarchal values but also as an empowering message for women to recognize their own strength and potential. Through education, participation in public life, and a commitment to nonviolence, women, Gandhi argues, can transform both themselves and society at large.

Choose the best answer:

1. According to Gandhi, what does the term "weaker sex" imply?

A) Women are physically inferior

B) Women are morally inferior

C) It is an unjust label imposed by men

D) Women are more emotional than men

2. What form of strength did Gandhi say women possess more than men?

A) Physical strength

B) Financial strength

C) Political strength

D) Moral strength

3. In Gandhi's view, which of the following traits is more pronounced in women than men?

A) Brute strength

B) Intuition

C) Aggression

D) Ambition

4.Gandhi believed that women excel in which of the following?

A) Endurance and self-sacrifice

B) Warfare and political leadership

C) Commerce and economics

D) Engineering and technical skill

5.What did Gandhi advocate for women's role in society?

A) To remain in traditional roles only

B) To step into public life and fight for independence

C) To focus solely on homemaking

D) To compete with men in physical labor

6.Gandhi's belief that women are not the weaker sex primarily focuses on their superior:

A) Physical capabilities

B) Intellectual achievements

C) Emotional stability

D) Moral and spiritual strength

7.Which social system did Gandhi oppose because of its unequal treatment of women?

A) Matriarchy

B) Patriarchy

C) Meritocracy

D) Democracy

8.Gandhi's views on women were most aligned with his broader philosophy of:

A) Capitalism

B) Nonviolence (Ahimsa)

C) Militarism

D) Technological advancement

9.According to Gandhi, which of the following was NOT a quality he believed women possessed?

A) Intuition B) Courage C) Aggression D) Self-sacrifice

10.Gandhi believed that labeling women as the "weaker sex" was:

A) A scientific fact B) A social injustice C) A religious belief D) A cultural tradition

TWO
THE FUN THEY HAD

· **ISAAC ASIMOV**

Margie even wrote about it that night in her diary. On the page headed May 17, 2157, she wrote, "Today Tommy found a real book!"

It was a very old book. Margie's grandfather once said that when he was a little boy his grandfather told him that there was a time when all stories were printed on paper. They turned the pages, which were yellow and crinkly, and it was awfully funny to read words that stood still instead of moving the way they were supposed to — on a screen, you know. And then, when they turned back to the page before, it had the same words on it that it had had when they read it the first time.

"Gee," said Tommy, "what a waste. When you're through with the book, you just throw it away, I guess. Our television screen must have had a million books on it and it's good for plenty more. I wouldn't throw it away."

"Same with mine," said Margie. She was eleven and hadn't seen as many telebooks as Tommy had. He was thirteen.

She said, "Where did you find it?"

"In my house." He pointed without looking, because he was busy reading. "In the attic."

"What's it about?"

"School."

Margie was scornful. "School? What's there to write about school? I hate school."

Margie always hated school, but now she hated it more than ever. The mechanical teacher had been giving her test after test in geography, and she had been doing worse and worse until her mother had shaken her head sorrowfully and sent for the County Inspector.

He was a round little man with a red face and a whole box of tools with dials and wires. He smiled at her and gave her an apple, then took the teacher apart. Margie had hoped he wouldn't know how to put it together again, but he knew how all right, and after an hour or so, there it was again, large and black and ugly, with a big screen on which all the lessons were shown and the questions were asked. That wasn't so bad. The part Margie hated most was the slot where she had to put homework and test papers. She always had to write them out in a punch code they made her learn when she was six years old, and the mechanical teacher calculated the mark in no time.

The Inspector had smiled after he was finished and patted her head. He said to her mother, "It's not the little girl's fault, Mrs. Jones. I think the geography sector was geared a little too quick. Those things happen sometimes. I've slowed it up to an average ten-year level. Actually, the overall pattern of her progress is quite satisfactory." And he patted Margie's head again.

Margie was disappointed. She had been hoping they would take the teacher away altogether. They had once taken Tommy's teacher away for nearly a month because the history sector had blanked out completely.

So she said to Tommy, "Why would anyone write about school?"

Tommy looked at her with very superior eyes. "Because it's not our kind of school, stupid. This is the old kind of school that they had hundreds and hundreds of years ago." He added loftily, pronouncing the word carefully, "Centuries ago."

Margie was hurt. "Well, I don't know what kind of school they had all that time ago." She read the book over his shoulder for a while, then said, "Anyway, they had a teacher."

"Sure they had a teacher, but it wasn't a regular teacher. It was a man."

"A man? How could a man be a teacher?"

"Well, he just told the boys and girls things and gave them homework and asked them questions."

"A man isn't smart enough."

"Sure he is. My father knows as much as my teacher."

"He can't. A man can't know as much as a teacher."

"He knows almost as much, I betcha."

Margie wasn't prepared to dispute that. She said, "I wouldn't want a strange man in my house to teach me."

Tommy screamed with laughter. "You don't know much, Margie. The teachers didn't live in the house. They had a special building and all the kids went there."

"And all the kids learned the same thing?"

"Sure, if they were the same age."

"But my mother says a teacher has to be adjusted to fit the mind of each boy and girl it teaches and that each kid has to be taught differently."

"Just the same they didn't do it that way then. If you don't like it, you don't have to read the book."

"I didn't say I didn't like it," Margie said quickly. She wanted to read about those funny schools.

They weren't even half-finished when Margie's mother called, "Margie! School!"

Margie looked up. "Not yet, Mamma."

"Now!" said Mrs. Jones. "And it's probably time for Tommy, too."

Margie said to Tommy, "Can I read the book some more with you after school?"

"Maybe," he said nonchalantly. He walked away, whistling, the dusty old book tucked beneath his arm.

Margie went into the schoolroom. It was right next to her bedroom, and the mechanical teacher was on and waiting for her. It was always on at the same time every day except Saturday and Sunday, because her mother said little girls learned better if they learned at regular hours.

The screen was lit up, and it said: "Today's arithmetic lesson is on the addition of proper fractions. Please insert yesterday's homework in the proper slot."

Margie did so with a sigh. She was thinking about the old schools they had when her grandfather's grandfather was a little boy. All the kids from the whole neighborhood came, laughing and shouting in the schoolyard, sitting together in the schoolroom, going home together at the end of the day. They learned the same things, so they could help one another with the homework and talk about it.

And the teachers were people...

The mechanical teacher was flashing on the screen: "When we add the fractions ½ and ¼..."

Margie was thinking about how the kids must have loved it in the old days. She was thinking about the fun they had.

Isaac Asimov's short story "The Fun They Had" was first published in 1951, and it provides a futuristic look at education and technology, with themes that resonate deeply in today's context of virtual learning and the digitization of education. Below is a detailed breakdown of the story, including an introduction to the author, a summary, themes, and an analysis suitable for a three-page overview.

Glossary:

1. Mechanical Teacher: A computer-based or robot-like teacher that instructs students individually. It contrasts with human teachers in traditional classrooms.
2. Crinkly: Describing something with a wrinkled or lined surface.
3. Scornful: Expressing contempt or disdain.
4. Geography: The study of the Earth, including landscapes, countries, and locations.
5. Arithmetic: A branch of mathematics that deals with numbers and calculations.

Notes:

Introduction to the Author: Isaac Asimov

Isaac Asimov (1920-1992) was one of the most prolific science fiction writers of the 20th century. Born in Russia and raised in the United States, Asimov is best known for his vast contributions to both science fiction and popular science writing. He wrote or edited over 500 books and is famous for works such as the *Foundation* series, *I, Robot*, and *The Gods Themselves*. Asimov's writings often explore the relationship between humans and technology, particularly focusing on how advancements in science and technology affect society, ethics, and the human condition.

In *The Fun They Had*, Asimov uses his characteristic foresight to imagine a world where education has become a highly personalized and automated process, raising questions about the role of human interaction and the value of traditional schooling.

Setting

The story is set in the year 2157, in a world where traditional schools no longer exist. Education is conducted at home through personalized machines called mechanical teachers. These teachers give lessons, assign homework, and assess students, all electronically.

Main Characters

Margie Jones: An 11-year-old girl who dislikes the robotic system of education. Margie's discontent is a central part of the story, reflecting her longing for something different.

Tommy: A 13-year-old boy who is Margie's friend. Tommy discovers a physical book, which is a rarity in their world where all reading is done on screens.

Plot Overview

The story begins with Tommy finding a dusty old book in the attic. Margie, who has never seen a physical book, is fascinated by the idea of printed pages. The book describes the traditional schooling system where students went to a school building, had human teachers, and studied together in classrooms. This concept is entirely alien to Margie and Tommy, whose education is isolated and conducted by mechanical teachers at home. Margie reflects on her own experience with her mechanical teacher, which has been difficult and frustrating, especially because it recently malfunctioned, requiring repair. Her mechanical teacher has been set to teach at a speed she finds too challenging, making her resent the entire learning process. As Margie listens to Tommy's descriptions of the old school system, she begins to imagine how fun it must have been for children to go to school, play together, and interact with human teachers. This sparks a sense of nostalgia for something she never experienced.

Ending

The story ends with Margie reluctantly returning to her lesson with the mechanical teacher, still thinking wistfully about the fun children must have had in the old days. The contrast between her dreary present and the seemingly joyful past remains unresolved, leaving readers to reflect on the nature of education and human connection.

Key Themes in "The Fun They Had"

· Technology and Education
· Nostalgia for the Past
· Isolation vs. Socialization
· Human vs. Machine
· The Nature of Learning

Analysis of "The Fun They Had"

Futuristic Vision and Present Relevance

Written in 1951, The Fun They Had offers a vision of the future that resonates with the present-day reality of online learning, digital classrooms, and virtual education tools. Asimov's foresight in predicting the rise of technology in education is striking, and the story invites readers to consider the implications of a highly automated educational system. The shift toward online and remote learning, particularly accelerated by events like the COVID-19 pandemic, makes Asimov's exploration of the pros and cons of technology in education especially timely.

Commentary on Human Interaction

At its heart, The Fun They Had is not just about education; it is about the human need for connection and socialization. The story suggests that while technology can enhance learning, it cannot replace the value of human relationships. Margie's curiosity about the old school system reflects a desire for something more meaningful and engaging than the mechanical routine of her lessons. This idea remains relevant today, as many educators and students grapple with balancing digital tools with in-person learning.

Margie's Nostalgia: A Critique of Modern Learning?

Margie's wistful thoughts about traditional schools can be read as a subtle critique of modern, tech-driven education systems. The emotional distance created by the mechanical teacher symbolizes the alienation that can come from an over-reliance on technology in learning. Asimov suggests that there is more to education than efficiency and convenience—there is a need for creativity, human connection, and the shared experience of learning.

The Role of the Book as a Symbol

The physical book that Tommy finds serves as a powerful symbol of the past. In a world dominated by screens, the book represents a tangible connection to history and tradition. Its discovery is a moment of awe for Margie and Tommy, who have only known digital forms of information. The book's presence in the story underscores the tension between old and new methods of learning and emphasizes the idea that while technology may advance, the value of certain traditional forms of education remains timeless.

Conclusion

Isaac Asimov's The Fun They Had presents a thought-provoking exploration of technology's role in education, human connection, and the impact of modern advancements on learning. Through Margie's longing for the past, Asimov invites readers to reflect on what might be lost in a world where human interaction is minimized and education is reduced to a mechanical process. The story's themes of nostalgia, isolation, and the nature of learning remain relevant in today's rapidly evolving educational landscape, making it a timeless piece of speculative fiction.

Choose the best answer:

1. Who are the main characters in The Fun They Had?

A) Margie and her mechanical teacher

B) Margie and Tommy

C) The County Inspector and Margie

D) Margie and her mother

2. What did Margie and Tommy find that fascinated them?

A) A telebook B) A new game C) An old physical book D) A map of the Earth

3. In which year is The Fun They Had set?

A) 2157 B) 2020 C) 3057 D) 2257

4. Why was Margie's mechanical teacher taken apart?

A) It was outdated B) It had stopped working entirely

C) It was giving her too many difficult geography lessons

D) It needed a software update

5. How did Tommy feel about traditional schools?

A) He thought they were boring B) He thought they were fun

C) He felt they were unnecessary D) He was indifferent

6. Where did Margie have her "school"?

A) In a school building B) In her bedroom C) In her mother's office

D) In the garage

7. What is a "telebook" in The Fun They Had?

A) A printed book with pages B) A tablet-like device used for reading

C) A television with lessons D) A virtual reality book

8. Why did Margie dislike school?

A) It was too hard B) She didn't like studying

C) She didn't like her mechanical teacher D) She preferred playing with friends

9. What does Margie imagine after reading about traditional schools?

A) Having friends to study with in a classroom

B) Learning from a newer, better mechanical teacher

C) Studying at home with family

D) A robot teaching all subjects

10. How did Margie feel about the old book they found?
A) She thought it was strange but interesting
B) She didn't care about it
C) She wanted to throw it away
D) She already knew everything in it

THREE

STOPPING BY WOODS ON A SNOWY EVENING

· **ROBERT FROST**

Whose woods these are I think I know.
His house is in the village though;
He will not see me stopping here
To watch his woods fill up with snow.

My little horse must think it queer
To stop without a farmhouse near
Between the woods and frozen lake
The darkest evening of the year.

He gives his harness bells a shake
To ask if there is some mistake.
The only other sound's the sweep
Of easy wind and downy flake.

The woods are lovely, dark, and deep,
But I have promises to keep,
And miles to go before I sleep,
And miles to go before I sleep.

Glossary

1. Queer- Strange or unusual.
2. Woods- A forested area or a collection of trees.
3. Frozen lake- A body of water that has solidified due to cold weather, turning into ice.
4. Downy flake- Soft, fluffy snowflakes.
5. Harness- The set of straps and fittings by which a horse is attached to a carriage or cart.

Notes:

Introduction to the Author: Robert Frost

Robert Frost (1874–1963) was an American poet celebrated for his depictions of rural life and the complex interplay between nature and human experience. His poetry often contains layers of meaning beneath seemingly simple descriptions, using natural scenes to explore philosophical and psychological themes. Frost won four Pulitzer Prizes for Poetry and became one of the most renowned and influential poets of the 20th century. Frost's work often reflects themes of isolation, decision-making, and the passage of time, while his language is marked by clarity and directness. One of his most famous poems, **"Stopping by Woods on a Snowy Evening,"** published in 1923 as part of his collection *New Hampshire,* exemplifies these traits with its evocative simplicity and deeper emotional undercurrents.

Themes:

- **Duty vs. Desire**
- **Isolation and Reflection**
- **Nature's Allure**
- **Life and Death**

Tone and Style:

- **Tone**: The tone of the poem is calm, meditative, and contemplative. There is a quiet peacefulness in the description of the woods, balanced by a sense of duty and restraint.

- **Style**: Frost's use of simple language and a regular rhyme scheme (AABA, BBCB, etc.) creates a musical quality. The straightforward diction masks the deeper philosophical meanings beneath the surface.

Symbolism:

The Woods: The woods symbolize the beauty and mystery of nature, as well as the temptation to escape from life's responsibilities. Their "darkness" and "depth" suggest that they could also represent the unknown or even death.

The Horse: The horse acts as a symbol of practicality and reality. While the speaker contemplates staying, the horse's confusion and impatience remind him of the obligations he must fulfill. The horse is a grounding force, representing the necessity to continue with life's tasks.

Snow: The snow in the poem creates a quiet, peaceful atmosphere, representing calmness and purity. It enhances the scene's tranquility, allowing the speaker a moment of pause to reflect on the surrounding beauty.

Summary and analysis

The poem begins with the speaker pausing by a set of woods on a snowy evening. He believes he knows the owner of the woods, who lives in a nearby village, and feels assured that no one will see him stop there. This opening sets up the speaker's sense of isolation and tranquility as he admires the quiet beauty of the woods filling up with snow. The use of the phrase "fill up with snow" captures the ongoing, gentle accumulation of snow, creating a peaceful, almost hypnotic atmosphere.

As the speaker continues to reflect on the scene, he considers how strange it might seem to his horse that they have stopped in a place without any human structures nearby, such as a farmhouse. The location is remote, lying between the woods and a frozen lake, and it is the "darkest evening of the year"—possibly the winter solstice, when the night is longest and darkness deepest. This adds a somber, almost mysterious quality to the scene, and it also emphasizes the speaker's isolation in this moment.

In the third stanza, the speaker notes that his horse shakes its harness bells, as if questioning whether there has been a mistake in stopping. The only other sounds are the soft wind and the gentle fall of snow. This contrast between the horse's restlessness and the peaceful silence of the natural world highlights the speaker's temporary pause in his otherwise purposeful journey.

In the final stanza, the speaker expresses how the woods are "lovely, dark, and deep." He is clearly captivated by the beauty and depth of the scene, which seems to pull him in, tempting him to linger longer. However, he acknowledges that he cannot stay. He has "promises to keep," and there are "miles to go before [he] sleep[s]." These lines emphasize

the pull of responsibility, reminding the speaker of his obligations. The repetition of the final line, "And miles to go before I sleep," reinforces the sense that the speaker must continue his journey, both literally and metaphorically.

Deeper Interpretations of the Summary

The poem portrays a simple moment—stopping to admire the beauty of snow-covered woods—but this moment takes on greater significance as it reflects the speaker's internal struggle. On the surface, it seems like a peaceful observation of nature, but as the speaker's thoughts deepen, the woods come to symbolize something more profound: the allure of rest, escapism, or perhaps even death.

The repetition of the final lines suggests that while the speaker is drawn to the serenity of the woods, he is fully aware of his responsibilities. The "promises" he must keep refer to commitments, both personal and social, that prevent him from giving in to the temptation of remaining in the peaceful stillness of nature. The "miles to go before I sleep" could be interpreted literally, meaning he has more distance to travel before he reaches his destination, or metaphorically, symbolizing the ongoing duties and tasks he must fulfill before he can rest, with "sleep" possibly hinting at the final rest—death.

Through this simple scene, Frost captures the tension between the speaker's desire for quiet reflection and the pressures of life. This balance between a moment of pause and the continuation of life's journey adds layers of meaning to the seemingly straightforward description of stopping by the woods on a snowy evening.

Multiple Choice questions:

1. What is the speaker's primary reason for stopping by the woods?

A) He is lost.

B) He wants to rest.

C) He is captivated by the beauty of the woods.

D) He is waiting for someone.

2. What is the rhyme scheme of each stanza in the poem, except for the last?

A) ABAB B) AABA C) AABB D) ABBA

3. What does the line "And miles to go before I sleep" imply?

A) The speaker is tired and needs to rest.

B) The speaker has a long journey ahead.

C) The speaker is dreaming.

D) The speaker has no destination in mind.

4. How does the speaker describe the woods?

A) Dark and dangerous

B) Bright and cheerful

C) Lovely, dark, and deep

D) Cold and gloomy

5. Why does the speaker mention his horse in the poem?

A) To show the horse is tired

B) To suggest that the horse does not understand why they are stopping

C) To describe his deep attachment to the horse

D) To indicate that the horse is scared of the woods

6. What season is it in the poem?

A) Spring B) Summer C) Fall D) Winter

7. What does the speaker mean by "He will not see me stopping here"?

A) The speaker is alone and feels unnoticed.

B) The speaker doesn't want to be seen by anyone.

C) The speaker knows the owner is away.

D) The speaker is hiding from someone.

8. In the line "The only other sound's the sweep / Of easy wind and downy flake," what is being described?

A) The silence and stillness of the woods B) A snowstorm in the woods

C) The sound of animals moving through the woods

D) The speaker's footsteps in the snow

9. What emotion does the speaker experience while watching the woods fill up with snow?

A) Fear B) Anxiety C) Awe and tranquillity D) Confusion

10. What is the underlying theme of the poem?

A) The beauty of nature versus the duties of life

B) Adventure and exploration

C) Friendship and loyalty

D) Wealth and success

FOUR

ODE TO SOLITUDE

-ALEXANDER POPE

Happy the man, whose wish and care
A few paternal acres bound,
Content to breathe his native air,
In his own ground.

Whose herds with milk, whose fields with bread,
Whose flocks supply him with attire,
Whose trees in summer yield him shade,
In winter, fire.

Blest, who can unconcernedly find
Hours, days, and years slide soft away
In health of body, peace of mind,
Quiet by day.

Sound sleep by night; study and ease,
Together mixt, sweet recreation,
And innocence, which most does please
With meditation.

Thus let me live, unseen, unknown,
Thus unlamented let me die,
Steal from the world, and not a stone
Tell where I lie.

Glossary

1. **Paternal Acres**: Land inherited from one's father or family.

2. **Native Air**: The air of one's homeland or country.
3. **Unconcernedly**: Without worry or care.
4. **Steal**: To move quietly and unnoticed.
5. **Unlamented**: Not mourned or grieved over.

Notes

In **"Ode to Solitude,"** Alexander Pope celebrates the simple, peaceful life of a person who is content living in harmony with nature, far removed from the chaos of society. The speaker praises the individual whose life is sustained by their own modest land, where they can breathe the air of their homeland and be self-sufficient. Their herds, fields, and flocks provide them with everything they need: food, clothing, and warmth. This person lives in a state of health, contentment, and peace of mind.

Pope emphasizes the blessings of a life where time passes gently, marked by good health and inner peace. The person enjoys the balance of work, study, and leisure, leading a life of innocence and reflection. Ultimately, the speaker expresses a desire to live and die

unnoticed, content to leave no grand legacy, slipping quietly from the world without even a gravestone to mark their final resting place.

Themes in "Ode to Solitude"

1. **Simplicity and Contentment:**

   ○ The poem celebrates a life of simplicity, where contentment comes not from wealth or fame but from self-sufficiency and being at peace with one's surroundings. The speaker finds joy in living off the land and enjoying nature's basic provisions.

2. **Solitude and Reflection:**

   ○ Pope praises the virtue of solitude, suggesting that time spent alone, away from societal distractions, leads to a life of peace and deeper reflection. Solitude allows the individual to focus on meditation, innocence, and quiet recreation.

3. **Self-Sufficiency**:

- The speaker lauds a life in which one's needs are met by their own land and resources. This self-sufficiency symbolizes a form of independence, both from others and from material excess.

4. **Peaceful Death**:

- The poem concludes with the speaker's wish to die unnoticed and without fanfare. The desire for a quiet death, without leaving a physical mark, reflects a contentment with life's transient nature and a rejection of the need for lasting recognition or fame.

5. **Time and Contentment**:

- The speaker imagines time passing effortlessly in a life lived in simplicity, free of worry. Time, measured not by grand achievements but by the smooth flow of days, highlights the theme of finding peace in the natural rhythms of life.

Choose the best answer

1. What is the central theme of "Ode to Solitude"?
A) The importance of wealth and fame
B) The beauty of nature and peace found in solitude
C) The value of hard work and societal success
D) The need for recognition and remembrance

2. What does the speaker mean by "a few paternal acres"?
A) Land acquired by hard work
B) Land inherited from the government
C) Land inherited from the family
D) A metaphor for spiritual wealth

3. Which of the following is NOT a source of contentment mentioned in the poem?
A) Wealth
B) Health of body
C) Peace of mind
D) Study and ease

4. What does the speaker wish for in death?

A) To be remembered with a grand monument

B) To have a small grave marker

C) To die unnoticed and unmarked

D) To be celebrated for his achievements

5. What does the phrase "slide soft away" refer to in the poem?

A) The passing of time without stress or worry

B) The melting of snow

C) A quiet, unnoticed death

D) A gradual descent into poverty

6. In the poem, what provides the speaker's clothing?

A) Wool from his flocks

B) Silk from distant lands

C) Cloth purchased from merchants

D) Leaves from the trees

7. What does the speaker primarily celebrate in "Ode to Solitude"?

A) Fame and fortune

B) The joy of a simple, peaceful life

C) The thrill of adventure

D) Friendship and love

8.According to the poem, what kind of land does the speaker prefer?

A) A large estate with many workers

B) A modest piece of land that he can work himself

C) A city apartment in a bustling area

D) A farm with many animals

9. What does the speaker suggest brings happiness and peace?

A) Wealth and luxury

B) Power and influence

C) Contentment and self-sufficiency

D) Travel and exploratio

10. How does the speaker describe the ideal life in the poem?

A) Full of social gatherings and excitement

B) Dedicated to public service

C) Quiet, secluded, and close to nature

D) Filled with ambition and goals

FIVE

THE CAT AND THE PAINKILLER

· **MARK TWAIN**

One of the reasons why Tom's mind had drifted away from its secret troubles was, that it had found a new and weighty matter to interest itself about. Becky Thatcher had stopped coming to school. Tom had struggled with his pride a few days, and tried to "whistle her down the wind," but failed. He began to find himself hanging around her father's house, nights, and feeling very miserable. She was ill. What if she should die! There was distraction in the thought. He no longer took an interest in war, nor even in piracy. The charm of life was gone; there was nothing but dreariness left. He put his hoop away, and his bat; there was no joy in them any more. His aunt was concerned. She began to try all manner of remedies on him. She was one of those people who are infatuated with patent medicines and all new-fangled methods of producing health or mending it. She was an inveterate experimenter in these things. When something fresh in this line came out she was in a fever, right away, to try it; not on herself, for she was never ailing, but on anybody else that came handy. She was a subscriber for all the "Health" periodicals and phrenological frauds; and the solemn ignorance they were inflated with was breath to her nostrils. All the "rot" they contained about ventilation, and how to go to bed, and how to get up, and what to eat, and what to drink, and how much exercise to take, and what frame of mind to keep one's self in, and what sort of clothing to wear, was all gospel to her, and she never observed that her health-journals of the current month customarily upset everything they had recommended the month before. She was as simple-hearted and honest as the day was long, and so she was an easy victim. She gathered together her quack periodicals and her quack medicines, and thus armed with death, went about on her pale horse, metaphorically speaking, with "hell following after." But she never suspected that she was not an angel of healing and the balm of Gilead in disguise, to the suffering neighbors.

The water treatment was new, now, and Tom's low condition was a windfall to her. She had him out at daylight every morning, stood him up in the woodshed and drowned him with a deluge of cold water; then she scrubbed him down with a towel like a file, and so brought him to; then she rolled him up in a wet sheet and put him away under blankets till she sweated his soul clean, and "the yellow stains of it came through his pores"—as Tom said.

Yet notwithstanding all this, the boy grew more and more melancholy and pale and dejected. She added hot baths, sitz baths, shower baths, and plunges. The boy remained as dismal as a hearse. She began to assist the water with a slim oatmeal diet and blister-plasters. She calculated his capacity as she would a jug's, and filled him up every day with quack cure-alls.

Tom had become indifferent to persecution by this time. This phase filled the old lady's heart with consternation. This indifference must be broken up at any cost. Now she heard of Pain-killer for the first time. She ordered a lot at once. She tasted it and was filled with gratitude. It was simply fire in a liquid form. She dropped the water treatment and everything else, and pinned her faith to Pain-killer. She gave Tom a teaspoonful and watched with the deepest anxiety for the result. Her troubles were instantly at rest—her soul at peace again; for the "indifference" was broken up. The boy could not have shown a wilder, heartier interest, if she had built a fire under him.

Tom felt that it was time to wake up; this sort of life might be romantic enough, in his blighted condition, but it was getting to have too little sentiment and too much distracting variety about it. So he thought over various plans for relief, and finally hit upon that of professing to be fond of Pain-killer. He asked for it so often that he became a nuisance, and his aunt ended by telling him to help himself and quit bothering her. If it had been Sid, she would have had no misgivings to alloy her delight; but since it was Tom, she watched the bottle clandestinely. She found that the medicine did really diminish, but it did not occur to her that the boy was mending the health of a crack in the sitting-room floor with it.

One day Tom was in the act of dosing the crack when his aunt's yellow cat came along, purring, eyeing the teaspoon avariciously, and begging for a taste. Tom said:

"Don't ask for it unless you want it, Peter."

But Peter signified that he did want it.

"You better make sure."

Peter was sure.

"Now you've asked for it, and I'll give it to you, because there ain't anything mean about me; but if you find you don't like it, you mustn't blame anybody but your own self."

Peter was agreeable. So Tom pried his mouth open and poured down the Pain-killer. Peter sprang a couple of yards in the air, and then delivered a war-whoop and set off round and round the room, banging against furniture, upsetting flower-pots, and making general havoc. Next he rose on his hind feet and pranced around, in a frenzy of enjoyment, with his head over his shoulder and his voice proclaiming his unappeasable happiness. Then he went tearing around the house again spreading chaos and destruction in his path.

Aunt Polly entered in time to see him throw a few double summersets, deliver a final mighty hurrah, and sail through the open window, carrying the rest of the flower-pots with him. The old lady stood petrified with astonishment, peering over her glasses; Tom lay on the floor expiring with laughter.

"Tom, what on earth ails that cat?"

"I don't know, aunt," gasped the boy.

"Why, I never see anything like it. What did make him act so?"

"'Deed I don't know, Aunt Polly; cats always act so when they're having a good time."

"They do, do they?" There was something in the tone that made Tom apprehensive.

"Yes'm. That is, I believe they do."

"You *better* believe they do! Yes, *you* better!"

Aunt Polly entered in time to see him throw a few double summersets, deliver

Glossary

1. **Painkiller**: A term used to describe a general medicine or tonic intended to relieve pain, but here it's used humorously to describe an ineffective and harsh home remedy.
2. **Patent medicine**: Over-the-counter medicinal products with exaggerated health claims, commonly sold in the 19th century without scientific backing.
3. **Ecclesiastical**: Related to the Christian Church; Tom uses the term while mimicking piety to get Aunt Polly's attention.
4. **Superstition**: Strong beliefs in things that are not based on science; Tom and other children in the story often display superstitious behaviors.
5. **Mischief**: Playful or mildly harmful behavior; Tom's mischief is shown in how he tricks his aunt and experiments with the Painkiller on the cat.

Notes:

Author Introduction

Mark Twain (1835–1910), born Samuel Langhorne Clemens, was an American writer, humorist, and social critic, often regarded as one of America's greatest authors. Known for his wit and keen observations of society, Twain's works capture the essence of small-town American life in the 19th century. The Adventures of Tom Sawyer and The Adventures of Huckleberry Finn are among his most famous novels, celebrated for their rich humor, adventure, and critical look at social norms and institutions.

Summary of The Cat and the Painkiller

In The Cat and the Painkiller, Tom Sawyer is feeling downhearted because Becky Thatcher, his crush, has stopped talking to him. Aunt Polly, noticing Tom's sadness, gives him various "remedies" to cheer him up. One of these is "Painkiller," a popular but dubious medicine. Tom dislikes the Painkiller but pretends to like it to avoid his aunt's suspicions. Eventually, Tom mischievously feeds the Painkiller to his aunt's cat, Peter, who reacts dramatically, causing chaos in the house. Aunt Polly discovers Tom's trick, scolds him, and eventually forgives him, bringing a bit of comic relief and showing Tom's playful, mischievous nature.

This chapter demonstrates Twain's humor and social commentary. Through Aunt Polly's faith in Painkiller, Twain humorously criticizes society's obsession with quick fixes and pseudo-remedies. The Painkiller episode reveals much about Tom's character: his playfulness, creativity, and occasional irresponsibility. Tom's choice to experiment on the cat reflects his innocent curiosity and the mischievous ways in which he copes with his emotional troubles. The chaotic results and Aunt Polly's reaction add a comical element, while also subtly showing the limits of parental and adult control over a child's natural rebellious spirit.

Twain's writing style—full of irony, satire, and humor—makes this episode both a funny story about childhood antics and a subtle critique of 19th-century society's reliance on pseudo-science. The exaggerated reaction of the cat to the Painkiller is a classic example of Twain's humor, as he often used animals and children to illustrate his points with exaggeration and wit.

Character Analysis

Tom Sawyer: Tom is mischievous and playful, with a rebellious streak that resists authority. He has a natural curiosity and often experiments with whatever he

1. encounters, showing both his resourcefulness and lack of foresight. His prank with the Painkiller on the cat highlights his sense of humor and disregard for rules when he is feeling low or wants attention.

1. Aunt Polly: A well-meaning but somewhat gullible figure, Aunt Polly loves Tom dearly and believes in traditional remedies, reflecting society's faith in dubious treatments of the time. Her reaction to Tom's antics shows her balance of strictness and affection; she scolds him but also cares deeply for him and is quick to forgive.

3. Peter the Cat: Though a minor character, Peter plays a crucial role in the comic escalation of the story. His exaggerated reaction to the Painkiller serves as a humorous climax and underscores Twain's satire of questionable remedies.

Themes

1. **Childhood and Mischief**

   Tom Sawyer's antics and mischievous behavior capture the essence of childhood curiosity and playfulness. This episode highlights how children often test boundaries and experiment in humorous or troublesome ways. Tom's experiment with the Painkiller on the cat shows a child's sense of fun but also a lack of understanding of consequences.

2. **Critique of Superstitions and Pseudoscience**

Twain satirizes the 19th-century obsession with "miracle cures" and patent medicines. Aunt Polly's belief in these remedies as solutions to Tom's emotional issues shows the period's reliance on dubious cures. Twain critiques how society placed misguided trust in these tonics, which were often ineffective or even harmful.

3. **Family and Discipline**

The story humorously reflects the relationship between Aunt Polly and Tom. She is both loving and gullible, genuinely concerned for Tom's well-being but prone to believing in pseudo-remedies. Their relationship balances discipline and affection, highlighting the familial dynamics of care and correction in a lighthearted way.

4. **Rebellion Against Authority**

Tom's trick with the Painkiller is an act of rebellion against Aunt Polly's strict regimen of health remedies. This moment shows Tom's desire to have control over his own body and decisions, subtly pushing back against the adult authority that prescribes treatments he finds unpleasant or unnecessary.

5. **Innocence and Guilt**

Despite Tom's trick on Aunt Polly, he feels some guilt for upsetting her and is relieved when she forgives him. This demonstrates his underlying good nature, even if his actions often get him into trouble.

Choose the best answer

1. Why does Aunt Polly give Tom various home remedies?

A) She believes they will improve his health.

B) She wants him to be quiet.

C) She is punishing him for misbehavior.

D) She's trying to make him study better.

2. What is Tom's emotional state at the beginning of The Cat and the Painkiller?

A) He is excited about a new adventure.

B) He is sad and heartbroken.

C) He is angry at Aunt Polly.

D) He is eager to go to school.

3. What is the Painkiller supposed to do for Tom?

A) Cure his sadness.

B) Relieve a stomach ache.

C) Help him sleep.

D) Stop his cough.

4. Why does Tom pretend to like the Painkiller?

A) He actually enjoys the taste.

B) He thinks it will make him feel better.

C) He wants to avoid Aunt Polly's suspicion.

D) He wants to get more of it.

5. Who does Tom decide to experiment on with the Painkiller?

A) His friend Joe Harper. B) Aunt Polly. C) Peter the cat. D) Becky Thatcher.

6. What is Peter's reaction after taking the Painkiller?

A) He falls asleep immediately. B) He purrs and relaxes.

C) He yowls and causes a commotion. D) He scratches Tom.

7. What lesson does Aunt Polly learn about Tom's "liking" for the Painkiller?

A) That he really does like it B) That he's been faking his enjoyment.

C) That it's been helping him. D) That he has been sharing it with friends.

8. How does Aunt Polly react when she finds out Tom gave Painkiller to the cat?

A) She is angry and punishes Tom severely.

B) She is amused but pretends to scold him.

C) She doesn't believe him at first.

D) She ignores him entirely.

9. Why did Tom give Peter the Painkiller?

A) He was curious about what would happen.

B) He thought it would help Peter.

C) He wanted to harm Peter.

D) Aunt Polly told him to.

10. What does Aunt Polly's reliance on the Painkiller suggest about her character?

A) She is easily tricked.

B) She deeply believes in folk remedies.

C) She doesn't care about Tom's health.

D) She wants to ignore Tom's emotions.

SIX

THE OPEN WINDOW

-H. H MUNRO

"My aunt will be down presently, Mr. Nuttel," said a very self-possessed young lady of fifteen; "in the meantime you must try and put up with me."

Framton Nuttel endeavored to say the correct something which should duly flatter the niece of the moment without unduly discounting the aunt that was to come. Privately he doubted more than ever whether these formal visits on a succession of total strangers would do much towards helping the nerve cure which he was supposed to be undergoing.

"I know how it will be," his sister had said when he was preparing to migrate to this rural retreat; "you will bury yourself down there and not speak to a living soul, and your nerves will be worse than ever from moping. I shall just give you letters of introduction to all the people I know there. Some of them, as far as I can remember, were quite nice."

Framton wondered whether Mrs. Sappleton, the lady to whom he was presenting one of the letters of introduction, came into the "nice" division.

"Do you know many of the people round here?" asked the niece, when she judged that they had had sufficient silent communion.

"Hardly a soul," said Framton. "My sister was staying here, at the rectory, you know, some four years ago, and she gave me letters of introduction to some of the people here."

He made the last statement in a tone of distinct regret.

"Then you know practically nothing about my aunt?" pursued the self-possessed young lady.

"Only her name and address," admitted the caller. He was wondering whether Mrs. Sappleton was in the married or widowed state. An undefinable something about the room seemed to suggest masculine habitation.

"Her great tragedy happened just three years ago," said the child; "that would be since your sister's time."

"Her tragedy?" asked Framton; somehow in this restful country spot tragedies seemed out of place.

"You may wonder why we keep that window wide open on an October afternoon," said the niece, indicating a large French window that opened on to a lawn.

"It is quite warm for the time of the year," said Framton; "but has that window got anything to do with the tragedy?"

"Out through that window, three years ago to a day, her husband and her two young brothers went off for their day's shooting. They never came back. In crossing the moor to their favourite snipe-shooting ground they were all three engulfed in a treacherous piece of bog. It had been that dreadful wet summer, you know, and places that were safe in other years gave way suddenly without warning. Their bodies were never recovered. That was the dreadful part of it." Here the child's voice lost its self-possessed note and became falteringly human. "Poor aunt always thinks that they will come back some day, they and the little brown spaniel that was lost with them, and walk in at that window just as they used to do. That is why the window is kept open every evening till it is quite dusk. Poor dear aunt, she has often told me how they went out, her husband with his white waterproof coat over his arm, and Ronnie, her youngest brother, singing 'Bertie, why do you bound?' as he always did to tease her, because she said it got on her nerves. Do you know, sometimes on still, quiet evenings like this, I almost get a creepy feeling that they will all walk in through that window—"

She broke off with a little shudder. It was a relief to Framton when the aunt bustled into the room with a whirl of apologies for being late in making her appearance.

"I hope Vera has been amusing you?" she said.

"She has been very interesting," said Framton.

"I hope you don't mind the open window," said Mrs. Sappleton briskly; "my husband and brothers will be home directly from shooting, and they always come in this way. They've been out for snipe in the marshes today, so they'll make a fine mess over my poor carpets. So like you menfolk, isn't it?"

She rattled on cheerfully about the shooting and the scarcity of birds, and the prospects for duck in the winter. To Framton it was all purely horrible. He made a desperate but only partially successful effort to turn the talk on to a less ghastly topic; he was conscious that his hostess was giving him only a fragment of her attention, and her eyes were constantly straying past him to the open window and the lawn beyond. It was certainly an unfortunate coincidence that he should have paid his visit on this tragic anniversary.

"The doctors agree in ordering me complete rest, an absence of mental excitement, and avoidance of anything in the nature of violent physical exercise," announced Framton, who laboured under the tolerably widespread delusion that total strangers and chance acquaintances are hungry for the least detail of one's ailments and infirmities, their cause and cure. "On the matter of diet they are not so much in agreement," he continued.

"No?" said Mrs. Sappleton, in a voice which only replaced a yawn at the last moment. Then she suddenly brightened into alert attention—but not to what Framton was saying.

"Here they are at last!" she cried. "Just in time for tea, and don't they look as if they were muddy up to the eyes!"

Framton shivered slightly and turned towards the niece with a look intended to convey sympathetic comprehension. The child was staring out through the open window with a dazed horror in her eyes. In a chill shock of nameless fear Framton swung round in his seat and looked in the same direction.

In the deepening twilight three figures were walking across the lawn towards the window; they all carried guns under their arms, and one of them was additionally burdened with a white coat hung over his shoulders. A tired brown spaniel kept close at their heels. Noiselessly they neared the house, and then a hoarse young voice chanted out of the dusk: "I said, Bertie, why do you bound?"

Framton grabbed wildly at his stick and hat; the hall door, the gravel drive, and the front gate were dimly noted stages in his headlong retreat. A cyclist coming along the road had to run into the hedge to avoid imminent collision.

"Here we are, my dear," said the bearer of the white mackintosh, coming in through the window; "who was that who bolted out as we came up?"

"A most extraordinary man, a Mr. Nuttel," said Mrs. Sappleton; "could only talk about his illnesses, and dashed off without a word of good-bye or apology when you arrived. One would think he had seen a ghost."

"I expect it was the spaniel," said the niece calmly; "he told me he had a horror of dogs. He was once hunted into a cemetery somewhere on the banks of the Ganges by a pack of pariah dogs, and had to spend the night in a newly dug grave with the creatures snarling and grinning and foaming just above him. Enough to make anyone lose their nerve."

Romance at short notice was her speciality.

Glossary

1. Rectory: The residence of a clergyman; in the story, it refers to the Sappletons' home.
2. Bog: A wet, marshy area, often difficult to navigate.
3. Romance: In older usage, this refers to an invented or exaggerated story.
4. Engulfed: To be completely surrounded or submerged by something.
5. Delusion: A false belief held despite evidence to the contrary.
6. Ghastly: Horrifying or shocking; often used to describe something that inspires fear or dread.
7. Infirmity: A physical or mental weakness, particularly one that affects someone's abilities.

Notes:

Author Introduction:

Saki, the pen name of British writer Hector Hugh Munro (1870–1916), is known for his witty, often darkly humorous short stories. His works frequently satirize Edwardian society, exposing the quirks and contradictions of upper-class life. The Open Window is one of his most famous stories, showcasing his talent for irony and surprise endings.

Themes

Deception and Manipulation

Vera's fictional story demonstrates her skill in manipulation, as she uses Framton's unfamiliarity with her family and environment to trick him. Her deception drives the plot, culminating in Framton's terrified escape.

Irony and Dark Humor

The story is structured around situational irony, where Framton's expectations and the truth are starkly different. Saki's humor lies in the contrast between Framton's assumptions and the reality, as well as Vera's cool response when her story is revealed as a prank.

Fragility of Human Perception

Framton's nervousness and preconceptions about the countryside make him vulnerable to Vera's deception. His need to interpret his surroundings without questioning reflects how our perceptions can be easily manipulated.

Innocence and Malice

Though young, Vera uses her storytelling ability to play on Framton's fears, presenting a contrast between innocence and malice. This theme questions the assumption that youth equates to purity or kindness.

Analysis

The Open Window is a masterfully crafted example of irony and the power of storytelling. Vera's character embodies the trope of the "unreliable narrator" in a uniquely manipulative way, as she creates a chilling story that plays on Framton's nerves. This technique showcases Saki's wit and his ability to create suspense with minimal action.

Saki also subtly critiques social conventions. Framton's visit, which was supposed to be therapeutic, becomes traumatic due to his unquestioning politeness and trust in strangers. Saki presents a humorous look at how adhering too strictly to social etiquette can make people vulnerable.

The story's ending is a sharp twist, revealing Vera as a clever trickster. Her composed lie about Framton's fear of dogs demonstrates her skill in controlling the narrative, exposing the vulnerability of human perception. Vera's quick improvisation at the end suggests that she often engages in such tricks, making readers question her true character. Saki's use of an open window as a focal point symbolizes both an entrance to new perspectives and a deceptive passage, as Framton sees it as a gateway to supernatural events that exist only in Vera's imagination.

Multiple-Choice Questions

1. Who is the protagonist of The Open Window?

A) Mrs. Sappleton B) Framton Nuttel C) Vera D) Mr. Sappleton

2. What condition is Framton Nuttel suffering from?

A) A heart problem B) A nervous condition C) Insomnia D) A leg injury

3. Who greets Framton when he arrives at the Sappleton home?

A) Mrs. Sappleton B) Mr. Sappleton C) Vera D) A servant

4. What story does Vera tell Framton about her aunt?

A) That her aunt lost her husband and brothers in an accident.

B) That her aunt is ill and rarely leaves the house.

C) That her aunt is afraid of the countryside.

D) That her aunt is a famous writer.

5. Why is the window kept open, according to Vera?

A) For fresh air.

B) In the hope that the missing family members will return.

C) To see the garden.

D) For the family dog to go in and out.

6. How does Framton react when he sees figures approaching the window?

A) He is relieved. B) He ignores them. C) He flees in terror. D) He greets them.

7. What is revealed about Vera at the end of the story?

A) She has a fear of dogs.

B) She often tells imaginative stories.

C) She had lost her family.

D) She dislikes strangers.

8. How does Mrs. Sappleton view Framton's sudden departure?

A) She is deeply offended. B) She is amused. C) She is confused. D) She is relieved.

9. What reason does Vera give for Framton's abrupt exit?

A) He saw a ghost.

B) He has a fear of dogs.

C) He remembered an appointment

D) He was feeling ill

9. What theme does the open window symbolize in the story?

A) Adventure B) Deception C) Freedom D) Hope

10. What literary device is used in the line, "Romance at short notice was her specialty"?

A) Simile B) Metaphor C) Irony D) Personification

SEVEN
ARTICLES

In English grammar, articles are words that define a noun as specific or unspecific. There are two types of articles: definite and indefinite.

1. Definite Article: "the"

"**The**" is used to refer to a specific noun that is already known to the reader or listener.

Examples:

- **The** book on the table is mine. (Referring to a specific book)
- I saw **the** movie you recommended. (Referring to a specific movie)

2. Indefinite Articles: "a" and "an"

"**A**" and "**an**" are used to refer to a non-specific noun.

"**A**" is used before words that begin with a consonant sound.

"**An**" is used before words that begin with a vowel sound.

Examples:

- I want to buy **a** car. (Any car, not a specific one)
- She is **an** engineer. (Any engineer, not a specific one)
- He has **a** unique perspective. (Referring to one of many possible perspectives)
- It was **an** interesting experience. (Referring to one of many experiences)

Note: Use "**the**" when talking about something specific.

Use "**a**" or "**an**" when talking about something non-specific.

Activity 1

Here are some sentences with blanks for you to fill in with the appropriate articles

("a," "an," or "the").

1. I saw ___ elephant at the zoo.
2. Can you pass me ___ salt, please?
3. She wants to be ___ doctor when she grows up.
4. Do you have ___ pen I can borrow?
5. ___ sun sets in the west.
6. He gave me ___ interesting book to read.
7. I need to find ___ job.
8. ___ Amazon River is the largest river by discharge volume.
9. There is ___ hour before the meeting starts.
10. She adopted ___ cat from the shelter.

Activity 2
Provide articles for the following words

1. Sun
2. Moon
3. Elephant
4. Flower
5. Student
6. Restaurant
7. Idea
8. Octopus
9. Earth
10. Umbrella

Activity 3
Answer the following questions

1. Give an example of a sentence using "a" and explain why you used it.
2. When would you use article "the" instead of articles "a" or "an"? Provide an example.
3. Can you explain why "an apple" is correct while "a apple" is not?
4. Create a sentence using "an" with a word that begins with a vowel sound.

5. Write a short paragraph (3-4 sentences) that includes at least three different articles.

EIGHT
CONCORDS

In grammar, **concord** refers to the agreement between words in a sentence, particularly in terms of number (singular or plural) and person (first, second, third).

Ten rules of concords

1. The verb and subject must agree in number (singular or plural)

This means that if the subject is singular, the verb should be singular and if the subject is plural, the verb should also be plural.
Examples:

1. He plays <u>football</u>. (Singular)
2. They play football. (Plural)

2. **Subjects that are joined by 'and' in a <u>sentence</u>, use a plural verb.**
Examples:

1. Radha and Meera are coming home.
2. Where are the pens and paper?

3. **Subjects that are joined by 'either/or', neither/nor' use a singular verb.**
Examples:
1. Neither Akshay nor Rohit is coming home.
2. My dad or my mom is arriving today

4. In sentences that include sums of money, periods of time or distances etc. (as a unit), use singular verbs.
Examples:

1. 500 rupees is a high price to pay.
2. 62 years is the minimum age of retirement.
3. 10 kilometres is too far to walk.

5. Nouns such as 'mathematics', 'civics', 'news' etc. while plural in form, are singular in meaning and use singular verbs.
Examples:

1. Mathematics is very difficult for some people.
2. The news is very saddening.

6. Sentences with pronouns such as anybody, anyone, no one, somebody, someone, everybody, everyone, nothing and nobody are treated as singular subjects and will therefore use a singular verb.
Examples:

1. Nobody has understood anything.
2. Everyone was happy with the outcome.
3. Nothing fits me well.
4. No one finds the movie interesting.

7. Abstract nouns and <u>uncountable nouns</u> are considered as singular subjects, so make sure you use a singular verb along with it.
Examples:

1. Honesty is the best policy.
2. Love makes people do crazy things.
3. Good friendship keeps your mind and body healthy.

8. When a sentence begins with 'each' or 'every' as the subject, it is considered singular and so the verb has to be singular too.
Examples:

1. Each student has been asked to provide a consent letter.

2. Every teacher and student is expected to work together.

9. Pronouns must agree with their antecedents (the nouns they refer to) in number, gender, and person.
Examples:

1. The boy lost his toy. ("boy" is singular and male, so the pronoun is "his")
2. The students forgot their books. ("students" is plural, so the pronoun is "their")

10. In a sentence, the verb tenses should logically agree to ensure clarity.
Examples:

1. She was reading when he arrived. (past continuous "was reading" aligns with past simple "arrived")
2. They have finished the project and now are relaxing. (present perfect "have finished" aligns with present continuous "are relaxing")

Activity 1
Choose the correct answers

1. The committee (decides/decide) on the new policy next week.
2. Each of the players (has/have) a specific role on the team.
3. Neither of the books (was/were) interesting to me.
4. The flock of sheep (is/are) grazing in the field.
5. Many a student (has/have) struggled with this topic.
6. Both of the girls (enjoy/enjoys) playing soccer.
7. Everyone in the class (has/have) submitted their assignments.
8. The family (is/are) going on vacation next month.
9. Either the cat or the dogs (is/are) making that noise.
10. A number of issues (was/were) discussed at the meeting.

Activity 2
Fill in the blanks
1. The noisy students _____ to leave after two warnings. (have/ has)
2. She is the only one of the students who_____ failed the test. (have/ has)
3. The crying _____ baby them. (irritate /irritates)
4. The longest of the presentations _____ the next group. (is/ are)

5. The students and their teacher _________ traveling to the competition. (is/ are)

6. Either one of the choices _______ going to disrupt the schedule. (is/ are)

7. This is the stereo system that ______ been purchased most often in our store (have/ has)

8. Nobody ______ to challenge the teacher when she is wrong. (dare/ dares)

9. The players or their coach _______ holding a press conference. (is/ are)

10. Neither of the students ______ been to Europe. (has/ have)

Activity 3

Answer the following

1. How does a verb agree with subjects joined by "and"?
2. What is the rule for subject-verb agreement with "either/or" or "neither/ nor"?
3. Do collective nouns take singular or plural verbs?
4. What are the rules for abstract nouns and uncountable nouns?
5. Write five sentences each using either – or, not only – but also, neither – nor.

NINE

ACTIVE AND PASSIVE VOICE

There are two voices:

1. Active

2. Passive

Look at the following sentences:

1. Ram wrote the novel.

2. The novel was written by Ram.

In the first sentence Ram, the 'doer' or the 'agent' is the subject of the verb 'wrote'. Here the verb is said to be in the 'active voice'.

In the second sentence, the 'doer' or the 'agent', Ram is not the subject of the verb 'wrote'. It is the object (novel) of the action which has been made the subject of the sentence. Here the verb is said to be in the 'passive voice'.

Active voice is often preferred in many types of writing due to its clarity, directness, and engagement. Here are some situations where active voice is especially effective:

1. **Expressing Clear Actions**: When you want the subject's action to be direct and easy to understand, active voice helps communicate it concisely.

   ○ Example: "The teacher explains the concept clearly."

2. **Making Writing More Engaging**: Active voice tends to feel livelier and more dynamic, making it ideal for storytelling, persuasive writing, and descriptions that need energy.

   - Example: "The team celebrated their victory with enthusiasm."

3. **Assigning Responsibility**: In sentences where it's important to know who is responsible for an action, active voice makes the subject (the doer) clear.

   - Example: "The manager approved the project on time."

4. **Providing Instructions or Commands**: In instructional or procedural writing, active voice is more straightforward, helping readers understand each step easily.

   - Example: "Add the sugar to the mixture."

5. **When Brevity is Important**: Since active voice tends to be more concise, it's often used when space is limited, such as in headlines, emails, or technical writing.

   - Example: "Researchers discovered a new species."

Passive voice can be useful in certain situations, especially when the focus is on the action or the object rather than on the subject. Here are some common situations where passive voice is effective:

1. **When the Doer is Unknown or Unimportant**: If the subject performing the action isn't known or is irrelevant, passive voice keeps the focus on the action or result.

   - Example: "The document was misplaced."

2. **When Emphasizing the Action Over the Doer**: Passive voice shifts attention to the action or object rather than the person performing it, which can be helpful in scientific, technical, or formal writing.

- ◦ Example: "The formula was tested multiple times."

3. **In Formal or Scientific Writing**: In academic and scientific writing, passive voice is often used to create a more objective tone, distancing the writer from the subject and focusing on data or results.

   - ◦ Example: "The experiment was conducted in a controlled environment."

4. **For Diplomatic or Polite Tone**: Passive voice can be used to soften statements, avoid assigning blame, or sound more polite, which is useful in sensitive communication.

   - ◦ Example: "Mistakes were made during the process."

5. **When Focusing on a Specific Part of a Sentence**: If you want to start a sentence with a particular noun (often the receiver of the action) to highlight it, passive voice can achieve this.

   - ◦ Example: "The final report was completed by the team."

Some more examples:
Active: They read the Ramayana daily.
Passive: The Ramayana is read by them daily.
Active: You are wasting your time
Passive: Your time is being wasted by you.
Active: The teacher punished him.
Passive: He was punished by the teacher.
Active: We shall play the match.
Passive: The match will be played by us.
Active: They grew rice.
Passive: Rice was grown by them.
Active: Mohan has completed his work.
Passive: His work has been completed by Mohan.
Active: He is exhibiting some paintings.
Passive: Some paintings are being exhibited by him.
Active: Mr. John sells radios.
Passive: Radios are sold by Mr. John.

When a sentence in the 'active voice' is changed into one in the 'passive voice', the following changes occur:

a. The 'object' of the verb in the 'active voice' becomes the 'subject' of the verb in the passive voice and the 'subject' in the 'active voice' becomes the 'object' in the 'passive voice'.

b. The main verb is changed into the 'past participle' (the third form) and an appropriate form of the verb "to be" (be, is, am, are, was, were, being, been) is put before it.

c. The 'subject' in the active voice (the doer of the action) becomes the 'object' in the passive voice and generally takes 'by' before it.

Activity 1
Change the sentences to passive voice

1. The cat chased the mouse.
2. The team won the championship.
3. She baked a delicious cake.
4. They painted the house blue.
5. The dog dug a hole in the yard.
6. He solved the puzzle quickly.
7. The musician played a beautiful melody.
8. The chef sliced the vegetables.
9. We celebrated her birthday at the beach.
10. The children built a sandcastle.

Activity 2
Change the sentences to active voice

1. The book was read by the entire class.
2. The letter was mailed yesterday by Sarah.
3. The concert tickets were sold out in minutes.
4. The meeting was postponed by the manager.
5. The homework was completed by the students.
6. The award was given to her for her achievements.
7. The building was designed by a famous architect.
8. The flowers were watered by the gardener.
9. The car was repaired by the mechanic.

10. The package was delivered this morning.

Activity 3
Answer the following questions

1. What is the main difference between active voice and passive voice in sentence structure?
2. Convert the following sentence from active to passive voice: "The company launched a new product."
3. Why might a writer choose to use the passive voice instead of the active voice?
4. Identify whether this sentence is in the active or passive voice: "The song was sung beautifully by the choir."
5. Change the following sentence to active voice: "The book was written by the famous author."

TEN
DIRECT AND INDIRECT SPEECH

The sentence spoken by a person can be reported in two ways. One way is to report the actual words of the speaker. This is called **direct speech**

Example: The boy said, "I want to play football this evening."

The verb 'said' in the above sentence is called the **reporting verb** and it is also the finite verb in the main clause. The actual words of the speaker are used here and so they are placed between inverted commas. There is also a comma used after the reporting verb.

The second way of reporting someone's words is to put them indirectly, that is, in the words of the reporter. This is called **reported speech or indirect speech.**

Example: The boy said that he wanted to play football that evening.

When we convert direct speech into indirect speech a few changes are made. In the above example, we made the following changes:

i.   The verb 'want' is changed into 'wanted'.
ii. 'This evening' is changed into 'that evening'.
iii. The pronoun 'I' becomes 'he'.
iv. The inverted commas are removed.

The following are some of the usual changes that take place when direct speech is changed into indirect speech.

Direct Speech	-	Indirect Speech
now	-	then
here	-	there
here after	-	there after
this	-	that
these	-	those
ago	-	before
thus	-	so
to-day	-	that day
to-night	-	that night
last night	-	the previous night
yesterday	-	the day before (or) the previous day
tomorrow	-	the next day (or) the following day
last week	-	the week before (or) the previous week
next week	-	the week after (or) the following week
last month	-	the month before (or) the previous month
next month	-	a month after

Figure 1

Questions in Indirect Speech

The verbs usually used to report questions are 'ask', 'enquire', 'demand' and 'want to know'.

Example:

He said, "Where are you going?"

→ He asked me where I was going.

"Where is the railway station", he enquired to me

→ He enquired to me where the railway station was.

Activity 1

Change the sentences to indirect speech

1. Sarah said, "I'm going to the store."
2. He asked, "Are you coming with us?"
3. "Please sit down," the teacher instructed.
4. My mom said, "Dinner will be ready in 15 minutes."
5. "I don't agree with that idea," he replied.
6. The manager announced, "The meeting starts at 10 a.m."
7. She whispered, "Don't tell anyone."
8. "Let's go to the beach tomorrow," John suggested.
9. The little boy shouted, "Look at me!"
10. "I've never been here before," Anna said excitedly.

Activity 2

Change the sentences to direct speech

1. He said that he would finish the project by Friday.
2. She told me that she had seen the movie last week.
3. The teacher explained that the test would cover chapters one to five.
4. My friend mentioned that they were planning a trip to Europe.
5. The doctor advised him to get more rest.
6. She asked whether I had completed my assignment.
7. They informed us that the event had been cancelled.
8. He remarked that it was going to rain later.
9. The coach urged the players to practice harder.
10. She expressed her hope that we would win the game.

Activity 3

Answer the following questions

1. What is direct speech, and how is it punctuated?
2. How do you convert a sentence from direct speech to indirect speech?
3. What are the key differences between direct speech and indirect speech?
4. What are some examples of reporting verbs used in direct and indirect speech?
5. When should you use indirect speech instead of direct speech?

ELEVEN
RESUME WRITING

Resume writing is the process of creating a structured document that outlines a person's professional history, skills, education, and achievements, tailored to the requirements of a specific job. A resume serves as a quick summary of a candidate's qualifications and is designed to persuade an employer to invite the applicant for an interview. Key sections typically include contact information, a summary or objective, work experience, education, skills, and relevant accomplishments.

How to format a resume

- Your resume must be well organized and easy to read.
- Choose an effective format and be consistent.
- Use bolds, italics, underlines, and capitalization to draw attention.
- List all relevant items in reverse chronological order in each section.

A strong resume should contain several key sections, each providing specific information to showcase your qualifications. Here are the essential elements to include:

1. Contact Information

- Full name
- Phone number
- Email address (use a professional-sounding email)
- LinkedIn profile or professional website/portfolio (optional, if relevant)

2. Professional Summary or Objective

- **Professional Summary**: A brief 2-3 sentence overview of your experience, skills, and what you bring to the position. Ideal for professionals with experience.
- **Objective**: A short statement about your career goals and how they align with the company's needs. Best for entry-level candidates or those changing careers.

3. Work Experience

- **Job Title**: Your position title.
- **Company Name and Location**: Include the company's name and location.
- **Dates of Employment**: Specify the months and years (e.g., "May 2019 – Present").
- **Achievements and Responsibilities**: List your responsibilities, emphasizing achievements with quantifiable results where possible (e.g., "increased sales by 30%").

4. Education

- **Degree and Major**: e.g., Bachelor of Science in Computer Science.
- **School Name and Location**: Name of the institution and its location.
- **Graduation Date**: Month and year (e.g., "May 2020").
- Relevant coursework, honors, or GPA (optional, if recent or relevant).

5. Skills

- A list of technical or professional skills relevant to the job, such as software proficiency, coding languages, or industry-specific tools. Use bullet points and keep it concise.

6. Certifications or Licenses (if applicable)

- Include any relevant certifications or professional licenses that demonstrate specialized skills or qualifications (e.g., "Certified Public Accountant," "Project Management Professional").

7. Projects or Portfolio Links (optional)

- If relevant, provide examples of past projects or a portfolio link, particularly for creative or technical fields. Briefly describe the project's goal, your role, and any outcomes.

8. Volunteer Experience (optional)

- Relevant volunteer work can showcase transferable skills and community involvement, especially for entry-level candidates or career changers.

9. Additional Sections (optional)

- **Languages**: List languages you speak and your proficiency level if they are relevant to the job.
- **Awards and Honors**: Mention any accolades that highlight your achievements.
- **Professional Affiliations**: List memberships in industry-related organizations or clubs.

Sample resume

SKILLS

Sales Management
Revenue Growth
Customer Service
Customer Needs Analysis
Conflict Resolution
Work Ethic & Professionalism
Effective Sales Process
Persuasive Selling Approach

EDUCATION

Associate of Arts in Business Administration
University of Alabama at Birmingham

LANGUAGES

English
Native or Bilingual Proficiency

Spanish
Professional Working Proficiency

French
Professional Working Proficiency

INTERESTS

Blockchain Technologies
Sailing
Web 3.0
Sustainability

Frank Graham
Sales Associate

Accomplished, growth-focused professional with 8+ years of dynamic sales experience across multiple industries. Equipped a steadfast commitment to customer service excellence to enhance customer experience, maximize satisfaction, propel retention, achieve/exceed sales goals, and increase business revenue. Possess superb abilities to develop and maintain a high level of product knowledge to persuasively promote them to existing and potential customers.

frank@novoresume.com
123 444 555
Montgomery, AL
linkedin.com/in/frank.g

WORK EXPERIENCE

Sales Associate
ShoPerfect Deluxe Mal
11/2018 - Present
Montgomery, AL
Achievements
Formulate and execute compelling seasonal sales promotions, resulting in over 30% increase in-store sales for five consecutive months in the year 2019 & 2023.
Proactively interact with customers to recommend products that best suit their tastes, interests, and needs, achieving a more than 98% in customer satisfaction rate.
Work collaboratively with a team of 8 other sales associates to devise strategic sales solutions to achieve and exceed the department's monthly, quarterly, and yearly sales goals.
Preserve up-to-date knowledge and information about the latest products or upcoming releases to effectively assist customers with various product-related concerns by providing accurate details.

Retail Sales Associate
Storefront Sports Solutions
01/2015 - 10/2018
Auburn, AL
Achievements
Devised and implemented an effective sales process, leading to consistently achieving the established sales goals and surpassing the monthly sales target by 12%.
Conceptualized and enforced a customer loyalty program that prompted both existing and new customers to purchase twice as much merchandise, resulting in a 50% increase in the department's sales.
Performed strategic upselling and cross-selling of women's apparel and other sports products based on customer's tastes and interests, which exceeded the yearly sales quotas by more than 10%.

CONFERENCES & COURSES

Sales Training for High Performing Team Specialization
Online Course - coursera.org

Practical Sales Management Training
ShoPerfect Deluxe Mall

Sales Training: Practical Sales Techniques
Online Course - udemy.com

Figure 2

Brooke Ware

Copywriter

Passionate and creative Copywriter **with 5+ years of writing experience**, skilled and experienced in SEO content writing, marketing, pitching, and developing a unique brand voice. Increased Burton Agency's user engagement on Facebook and Instagram by 34% in 4 months, resulting in an 18% increase in sales.

 brooke@novoresume.com   123 444 555   Columbus, Ohio   medium.com/@brooke.ware

WORK EXPERIENCE

Lead Copywriter
Burton Agency

01/2019 - Present

Achievements

- Consistently wrote a minimum of 7 Facebook and Instagram posts per week, which helped to grow the Facebook follower base from 6,000 to 90,000+ and the Instagram follower base from 3,000 to 160,000+ users in 5 months.
- Increased user engagement on Facebook and Instagram by 34% in 4 months.
- **Helped to boost product sales by 18% in 4 months** to over $150.000.
- Wrote weekly newsletters to an audience of 50,000+ readers.
- Developed a unique brand voice for the company and used it consistently across all platforms, including social media posts, newsletters, and the brand website.

Copywriter
Think Co.

05/2016 - 12/2018

Achievements

- Rewrote 10+ landing pages, leading to a 28% increase in landing page conversions in 6 months.
- Wrote 3 SEO blog articles each week in English and Spanish languages for a total of 100,000+ readers.
- **Increased organic traffic by over 60%** in a year.
- Edited all material to ensure it conforms to the company's branding standards.
- Assisted graphic designers to ensure the consistency and accuracy of copy across all materials.

EDUCATION

BA in Journalism (Minor in Marketing)
The Ohio State University

09/2013 - 06/2016

GENERAL SKILLS

Copywriting	Establishing Tone
Identifying Audience	Wordpress
SEO	Digital Marketing
Attention to Detail	Time-management
Creative Writing	Editing

PERSONAL PROJECT

Freelance Fiction Writer (2016 - Present)

- Compose fiction or nonfiction prose, such as short stories, novels, articles, descriptive or critical analyses, and essays.
- Develop story influences such as themes, plots, characterizations, psychological analyses, historical environments, action, and dialogue to create material ensuring efficiency of the creative process to deliver the project on time.
- Prepare drafts in the correct, readable format for publication and send them to publishers or producers.
- Revise the written material to satisfy the needs of clients, publishers, directors, or producers.
- Confer with clients, editors, publishers, or producers to discuss changes or revisions to written material.

LANGUAGES

English
Native or Bilingual Proficiency

Spanish
Native or Bilingual Proficiency

French
Full Professional Proficiency

German
Limited Working Proficiency

INTERESTS

- Renewable Energy
- Gardening
- Caligraphy
- Astronomy

Figure 3

Activity 1

1. Create a resume of your own.

2. How to format a resume attractively?

3. What are the informations to be added on a resume?

TWELVE
EMAIL WRITING

Email is a very specific form of communication—it is a quick, inexpensive and convenient way of communicating with a small or large audience, who may be next door or across the world. It is a great way to make arrangements—provided that they are not urgent. Instant delivery does NOT mean the recipient will read it immediately. It is an excellent way to get information to a wide range of people— as long as your subject line is relevant or interesting enough to get them to read it. It is a simple way of asking for a response—as a follow up, not as a long explanation and request for action. It is a wonderful way to send information—as attachments not in the body of the email. An email is not a letter, a report or the minutes of a meeting—but it is an excellent way of sending information to an audience, or asking for a response.

Structure of emails

Emails are by far the most common method of communication for internal office correspondence, and they are fast replacing letters in all but the most formal business situations. Most people in companies use emails for a wide range of purposes: to confirm appointments and meetings, request help or action, provide information, etc.

Here is the explanation of some terms you will come across while composing a new email message:

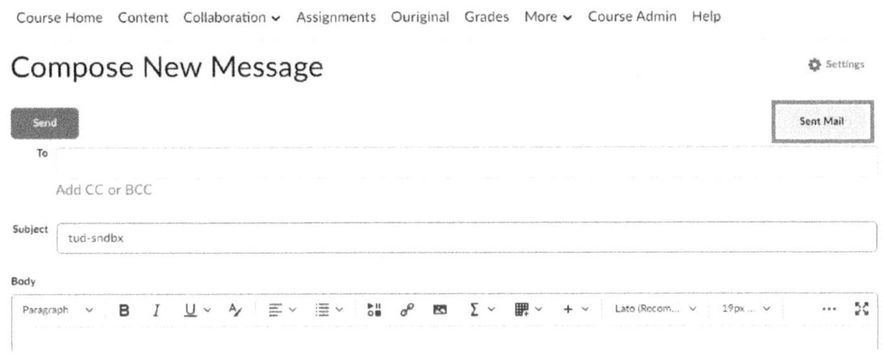

Figure 4

To: this line is for providing the address of the person you are mailing to.

Subject: this is for providing the title of the message. It should be brief.

Cc: you can enter an address here to send a copy of a mail to someone else other than the person to whom you are mailing.

Bcc: it means blind copy. As with the cc line, a copy of the message will be sent to the address you provide in the Bcc line. However, the recipient of the original message will not be able to tell that the Bcc address received a copy.

Attachments: this option is to attach and send files on the computer along with the message.

The big blank area: this is where you type your message (body of the text)

Guidelines for writing emails

Be brief

Get straight to the point with your reason for writing. Edit carefully so that your email contains only the most important information. Less important information can be sent in a separate email.

Be clear

Use a descriptive subject line that tells your reader what your email is about. If necessary, change the original subject line if it's too vague or if the conversation has moved on to other areas.

Plan

For longer emails, a plan helps you focus on the objective of your email and keeps your ideas linked and concise.

Be accurate

Use your spell check to eliminate spelling or typing errors.

Delete previous emails

Delete original emails if they are long or unconnected to your present email. Instead, refer to parts of the previous email with angle bracket keys: < and > or << and >>

Use a plain background

It is better to use black text on white background to be sure that your email is easy to read. Patterns or motifs in the body of the email risk making you look childish or immature – stick to a plain white background.

Be polite

Avoid writing sarcastic or angry comments. It's far better to delay sending an email until after you've had time to cool off than send something you might later regret.

Starting an email

You don't need to write "Dear ..." at the beginning of the email, especially if you are writing to people within your company. As the name of the person, you are writing to appears in the *To:* box of the email, you can start writing your message immediately.

Ending an email

There are a variety of ways to end your email. If you start with "Dear..." you can choose one of the endings used also in letters:

The email starts "Dear Mary".

The email ends with "Best wishes" or "Kind regards". The email starts "Dear Mr. Johnson".

The email ends "Yours sincerely" or "Sincerely" in American English.

If your email did not start with "Dear" and a name, then you can use any of these endings:

"Best wishes" "Thanks"

"Thanks and regards" "Kind regards" "Yours"

Activity 1

1. Prepare an email to inform the class tutor that you are not keeping well and hence you will not be able to attend the class for the next three days.
2. Prepare an email to the Manager of the Bank that you have an account. You want to get the monthly statement of transactions via email. Request him/her to do the same.

THIRTEEN
DIALOGUE WRITING

Dialogue writing is the creation of a conversational exchange between two or more characters. It's often used in storytelling, plays, novels, and scripts to reveal characters' personalities, advance the plot, or convey emotions and information indirectly through speech.

Sample Dialogues:

Friends Planning a Vacation

Lily: "So, where should we go this summer? I was thinking somewhere by the beach."

Sam: "Beach sounds great, but what about trying something new? Like a hiking trip in the mountains?"

Lily: "Hiking could be fun. But can we at least find a place with a lake? I still want to go swimming!"

Sam: "Perfect! A lake with mountain trails nearby would be the best of both worlds."

Lily: "Agreed. Let's start looking up places tonight!"

Teacher and Student Discussing Grades

Teacher: "I noticed that your grade on the last test wasn't as high as usual. Is everything okay?"

Student: "Honestly, I was really overwhelmed with assignments from other classes. I tried my best, but I couldn't focus."

Teacher: "I understand. Balancing everything can be tough. Would you be interested in some extra practice materials? I think it might help you catch up."

Student: "Yes, that would be great! I want to do better on the next test."

Teacher: "Good to hear. I'll send some practice problems your way."

Activity 1

1. Write a dialogue between you and customer care executive regarding poor network coverage in your area.

2. Write a dialogue between doctor and patient regarding health concerns.

FOURTEEN

TESTIMONIAL WRITING

Figure 5

Testimonial writing is the process of creating a short, written statement that expresses a person's positive experience with a product, service, company, or individual. Testimonials are often used in marketing and business contexts to build trust, credibility, and social proof by showcasing satisfied customers' feedback. A testimonial typically includes specific details about how the product or service benefited the person and why they recommend it to others.

Key Elements of a Good Testimonial

1. **Specificity**: It's impactful when a testimonial highlights specific features, results, or qualities that made a difference.
2. **Personalization**: Including the person's name, role, or company (with permission) makes the testimonial more relatable and credible.
3. **Authenticity**: Honest, natural language often has a greater impact than highly polished or formal wording.
4. **Benefit-Oriented**: Focusing on how the product or service solved a problem or improved the customer's situation resonates with potential buyers.

Sample testimonials:

1. Product Testimonial (Fitness Equipment)

"I purchased the FitPro Resistance Bands a month ago, and they have completely transformed my home workout routine. The quality is outstanding, and the variety of resistance levels allows me to challenge myself every day. I've already noticed significant improvements in my strength and flexibility. Highly recommend!"
— Mark Johnson, Fitness Enthusiast

2. Service Testimonial (Digital Marketing Agency)

"Working with Creative Solutions Marketing has been a game-changer for our business. Their team developed a targeted social media strategy that increased our engagement by over 50% in just three months. Their insights into consumer behavior are invaluable. I can't thank them enough!"
— Sarah Lee, Owner of Trendy Boutique

3. Education Testimonial (Online Course)

"The Graphic Design Bootcamp was exactly what I needed to kickstart my career. The course was comprehensive, and the instructors were

knowledgeable and supportive. By the end, I had built an impressive portfolio that helped me land my first design job. I couldn't be happier!"
— Emily Tran, Recent Graduate

Activity 1

1. Write a testimonial for a travel agency mentioning about a recent trip.

2. Write a testimonial on healthcare which you recently visited. (eg: physical therapy clinic etc...)

9 798896 322030